# THREE LINKS HIJINKS
## AN ODD FELLOW'S JOKE BOOK

WRITTEN BY
**IAN LOVE-JONES**
ILLUSTRATED BY
**SARAH KEENA**

Copyright © 2025 by Ian Love-Jones

Edited By David Scheer

Illustrations copyright © 2025 by Sarah Keena

All rights reserved. No portion of this book may be reproduced in any form without written permission from the publisher or author, except as permitted by U.S. copyright law.

First Edition: June 2025

ISBN 978-1-962533-02-7

Are you an Odd Fellow — a member of our specific fraternal order that focuses on universal kinship, friendship, love, and truth, and acts of charity?

Even if you aren't – keep reading! You don't **have** to be a member of a "secret" society to find this book funny. If you'd *like* to become an Odd Fellow though – go for it! As an Odd Fellow, you will find this book 35% funnier knowing the quirks, jargon, subgroups, and subtext from our friendly society.

Being an Odd Fellow isn't all solemn obligations, secret handshakes, and weighty ceremonies. Just as often, thankfully, Odd Fellowship is about humans from different walks connecting around a shared desire to do good, and to enjoy each other's company in the process.

What better way to connect folks from different walks of life, than through the universal language of humor. I hope you enjoy all of the three links hijinx!

In FL&T,

Me (Ian Love-Jones)

Q: Why did the Noble Grand ask about specials at the diner?

A: He didn't see the counter sign.

Q: Why did the Wardens open up a burger joint?

A: They knew how all the shakes were made.

**Q: What's the best card to have in a game of Odd Fellow's poker?**

**A: A dues card.**

**Q: Where's the best place to play poker with an Odd Fellow?**

**A: In the Ante Room!**

Q: Which officers are most likely to start a band?

A: The Musician, the Conductor and the Recording Secretary.

Q: What's an Odd Fellow skydiver's favorite kind of story?

A: A parable.

Q: Where do you find dad jokes on an Odd Fellow's camping trip?

A: In the Patriarch's Silly-tent.

Q: Where do Muscovites and Samaritans get their hats?

A: From a Fez dispenser.

Q: Why didn't the bank robber go to Lodge?

A: He heard the Warden was there.

Q: What do you call not eating before you swim?

A: The Golden Rule of en-cramp-ment.

Q: What's a Rebekah's favorite hairdo.

A: The Beehive.

Q: Why did the Muscovite buy an anniversary gift?

A: For the wife of the Czar!

**Q: Why was the Warden's wife angry?**

**A: He didn't collar.**

**Q: What was the Guardian's favorite kind of humor?**

**A: Knock-knock jokes.**

**Q: What did the Noble Grand say when they found barbecue sauce in the ballot box?**

**A: "I find this ballot flavor-able."**

**Q: Why was the Warden so well informed?**

**A: He axed a lot of questions.**

Q: What is the obligation of an Odd Fellow comedian?

A: To visit the schtick!

Q: Why did the veteran Odd Fellow need a fan?

A: Too many degrees.

Q: Where did the Guardians get their education?

A: The school of hard knocks.

Q: What was the swashbuckler's favorite Lodge office?

A: Treasurer.

Q: How did the twins pass every motion?

A: They were always seconded.

Q: Why did the Vice Grand have such comfortable shoes?

A: Good Supporters.

Q: What do you call it when people stare at your regalia?

A: A chain reaction.

Q: Why did the degree team get in trouble?

A: They were always making a scene.

**Q: Why did the Financial Secretary get paid?**

**A: His name was Bill.**

**Q: Why couldn't the Odd Fellows knock down any bowling pins?**

**A: Too many odd balls.**

**Q: Why did the Odd Fellow walk around with marshmallows and a sleeping bag?**

**A: They were looking for the Encampment.**

**Q: What sound does an Odd Fellow make when they stub their toe?**

**A: I oof!**

Q: What do you call an Odd Fellows' undersea youth group?

A: They da Roe.

Q: Why did the Odd Fellow termites get all of their degrees?

A: So they could go to Grand Logs.

Q: What's a dog's favorite degree in Odd Fellowship?

A: Royal Pup-ple.

Q: How did the Muscovites get to the Lodge?

A: They rode the busby.

**Q: Why didn't the Musician use an old piano?**

**A: Past Grands need some rest.**

**Q: Why didn't the Odd Fellows take a seat?**

**A: They wanted to be in good standing.**

Q: Why didn't the Odd Fellow make it into Lodge?

A: He couldn't get a grip.

Q: What's the difference between a Good Samaritan, and a So-so Samaritan?

A: The So-so Samaritan will stop ... after they run a few errands.

Q: Who did the hungry Odd Fellow bring to the dance as a +1?

A: Refreshments.

Q: How did the Conductor know what they were getting for the Holidays?

A: They examined all present.

Q: What's an Odd Fellow's favorite breakfast?

A: Three links.

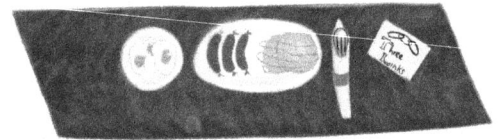

# THREE LINKS HIJINKS

**Q: Why was the Odd Fellow's bakery empty?**

**A: They always buried the bread.**

**Q: Why did the Odd Fellow's dog go out to the yard?**

**A: To visit the stick.**

**Q: Why did the unicycle become an Odd Fellow?**

**A: To promote harmony and good wheel.**

**Q: What do Odd Fellows and fishermen have in common?**

**A: The network.**

Q: Did you hear about the initiate who leveled up at the laundromat?

A: He forgot to take that red sock out of the wash.

Q: Why did the detective look into the Encampment?

A: He heard there were crooks on the emblem.

**Q: What's the best place to put a Chevalier's drink?**

**A: In the CANton.**

**Q: Why did the Chevaliers replace their Captain?**

**A: He kept bringing a phaser to all of the meetings.**

**Q: What are an Odd Fellow's two favorite things to draw?**

**A: A tattoo, or a pension!**

**Did you hear about the disco dancing Chaplain?**

**The members united with the Chaplain in flair.**

**Q: Which officer talks to members behind on their dues?**

**A: The Bad-News Bearer.**

**Q: How do belly buttons enter the lodge?**

**A: Through the innie door.**

Q: What do gavels and late members have in common?

A: They both rap.

Q: What's a Muscovite's favorite sports team?

A: The Bears!

Q: Why did the 2nd Degree Odd Fellow like the simpler things?

A: He was a blue-collar Joe.

**Q: What do you call two Odd Fellows who look alike?**

**A: Fraternal twins.**

**Q: Why did the Odd Fellow put a gumball in the ballot box?**

**A: She wanted to chew on the matter a little longer.**

An Odd Fellow's kid asked, "Dad, what month was I born in?"

The Odd Fellow smiled and replied "not May son."

Q: What is the motto of Odd Fellow fireflies?

A: Ask me, I may glow.

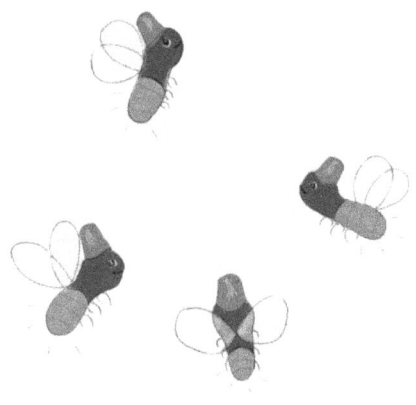

**Did I tell you how I knew the bank teller was an Odd Fellow?**

**I asked to make a big withdrawal and she shouted "be at once, undeceived!"**

**Q: What is the motto of Odd Fellows Dentists?**

**A: Friendship, Love and Tooth.**

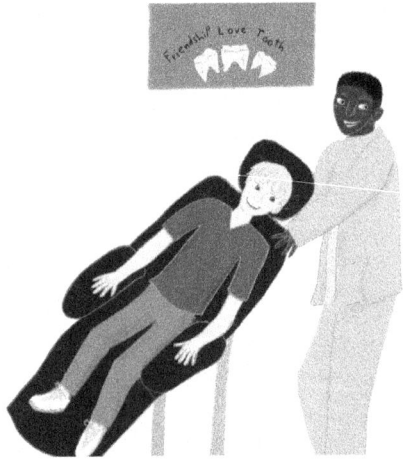

Q: Which Supporter is correct during an argument?

A: The Right Supporter!

Q: What does an Odd Fellow call wearing many hats?

A: The Sign of Recognition.

**Q: Why did everyone come to the Odd Fellow's tavern?**

**A: It had Seven Stars.**

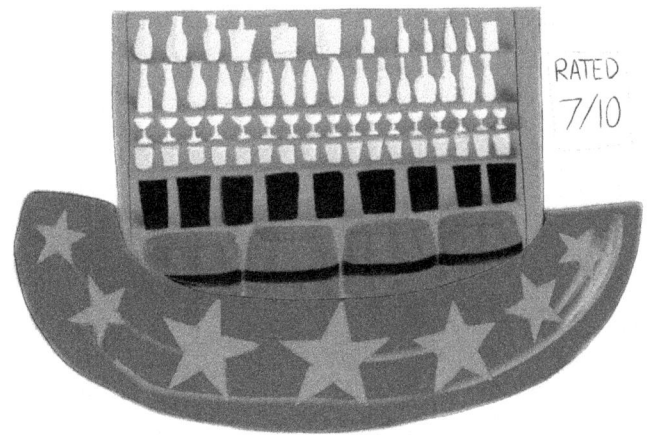

**Q: Why did members move to pay the Lodge bills?**

**A: The bills were on the other side of the room.**

Q: What do Odd Fellows call a sign-up sheet?

A: Deja vu.

Q: What kind of birds are strongest together?

A: A bundle of chicks.

**Q: Why did the Odd Fellows lift donations above their heads?**

**A: They enjoyed fund-raising.**

**A man walked up to an Odd Fellow and said "I hear your Lodge has skeletons in it's closet."**

**The Odd Fellow replied, "We've never needed more than one skeleton, but I guess it wouldn't hurt to have a spare."**

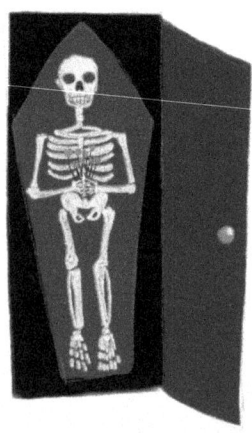

**Q: Why did the busbies get tangled together?**

**A: There was a tassel hassle.**

**Q: What's it called when an Initiatory Degree member won't bring snacks?**

**A: White-collar crime.**

**An Odd Fellow walked into a Sanctorum and asked "Why is this place filthy?"**

**A Samaritan looked up from his newspaper and answered, "Because we never sweep."**

Q: Why did the Odd Fellow put groceries behind the steering wheel?

A: To set up a canned food drive.

Q: Why did the Warden's axe need fixing?

A: It wouldn't take credit cards.

After inspecting the ballots the Vice Grand said "Why is there a note in the ballot box saying buy better cake?"

Looking embarrassed, a new member piped up "Ballot box? Sorry, I thought that was the suggestion box!"

Q: How can you tell a Muscovite's busby from a Samaritan's fez?

A: Different secret hat-shakes.

Q: Why did the boats become Odd Fellows?

A: For fellow-ship.

Odd Fellow 1: Do you know who just sent all those kids upstairs in the elevator?

Odd Fellow 2: Yeah that was me. We're supposed to elevate the orphans, remember?

Q: What's the motto of Odd Fellow horses?

A: Memento More Hay.

**Q: What's the motto of an Odd Fellow fish?**

**A: Carpe Diem.**

**Q: What's a detective's favorite degree in Odd Fellowship?**

**A: The 3rd Degree.**

Q: What does the I.O.O.F. have in common with a forgetful baker?

A: They both lost the apron.

The handyman rushed over to an Odd Fellow and blurted out, "I think your building is haunted! I heard footsteps upstairs during the overnight job."

The Odd Fellow smiled and said "Oh no, that's just our Recording Secretary, he never leaves."

Q: How do Odd Fellows clean the bathroom?

A: According to Robert's Rules of Odor.

**Q: Why can't Odd Fellows wear costumes at the table?**

**A: If a helmet falls off, it might spike the punch.**

**Q: How is an Odd Fellows Lodge like an old motel?**

**A: They both have a registry, lots of old robes, and at least one guest rattling around.**

**Q: What do you call a party at the Sanctorum?**

**A: A fez-tival.**

**A sunbather was relaxing on the beach when an Odd Fellow marched up and shouted "My turn!"**

**When the sunbather looked confused, the Odd Fellow explained, "I have strict orders to relieve the de-stressed."**

Q: Why did the maple, the oak, and the dogwood become Odd Fellows?

A: They valued the tree links.

Q: Why did the candidate stare at the brochure?

A: To learn the dues and don'ts.

Q: Why did the Odd Fellows take so long to leave?

A: They couldn't remember the bye-laws.

Q: When did the new Officer get stuck in the ceiling?

A: At the installation ceremony.

Q: Why does the Warden get into any party they want?

A: They have an all axes pass.

Q: What's an Odd Fellow's favorite bedding?

A: Sign up sheets.

Q: Why did the Noble Grand always beat the Right Supporter at whack-a-mole?

A: The Noble Grand had twice as many hammers.

Q: Which Odd Fellow did best at the eye exam?

A: The all-seeing guy.

Q: What's the motto of the small Odd Fellow Lodge?

A: The smaller the crew, the more you must do!

Q: What's the motto of the big Odd Fellow Lodge?

A: We have more members, the votes take forever!

Q: Why were the Vice Grand's offices so popular?

A: That hourglass looks like a bowling pin!

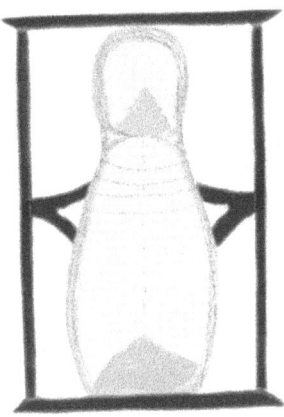

**Q: Why did the Big Bad Wolf try to join the Odd Fellows?**

**A: He wanted heart n' ham.**

**Q: What do you call a fish with a grand vision about Friendship, Love, and Truth?**

**A: The flounder of Odd Fellowship.**

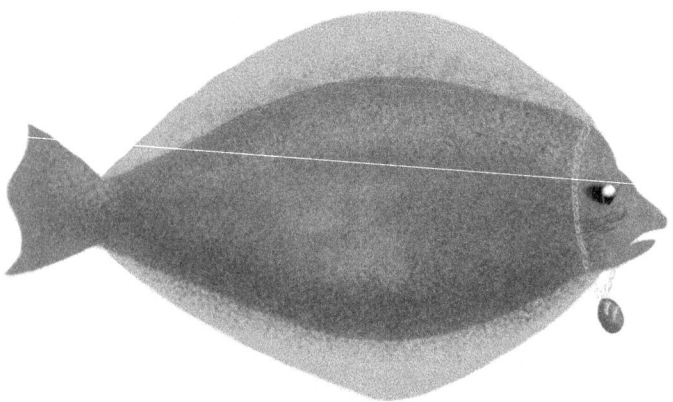

# About the Author

Ian Love-Jones is an Odd Fellow (and Muscovite) from Peninsula lodge #128. Like most Odd Fellows, he wears many hats.

Ian is a creative, a voiceover talent, an educator, and a former Corrections Sgt.

He's also a happy husband and a proud dad (which should explain all of the dad-jokes in this book)!